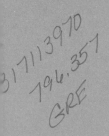

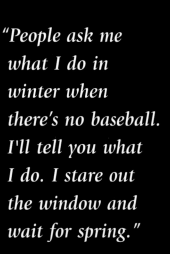

"People ask me what I do in winter when there's no baseball. I'll tell you what I do. I stare out the window and wait for spring."

—Rogers Hornsby

101 Reasons to Love the
CARDINALS

Ron Green, Jr.

Stewart, Tabori & Chang
New York

Introduction

Among the beautiful things about baseball—beyond the way the field lays and the sound of a wooden bat on a ball—is the way it's shared by families and friends and a nation.

It's why the St. Louis Cardinals don't belong only to the good people who live in the shadow of the Gateway Arch but to those who spent their summer evenings tuning in to the crackling broadcast on KMOX where Jack Buck's voice stitched together a community thousands of miles wide.

It's why a father and son like Randy and Paul Gardner could live in North Carolina and come to care about the Cardinals the way they would the family dog or their best friends from childhood.

Beyond their natural ties, there is the bond of baseball, specifically Cardinals baseball. Paul would listen to his father talk about Stan Musial, hear the passion, and it became a part of him. With children of his own now, Paul shares the Cardinals with them the way his father shared with him.

They are just one family among so many who feel the same away about the Cardinals. They are spread like sunshine across the land, giving a special light to a franchise that's a part of their family.

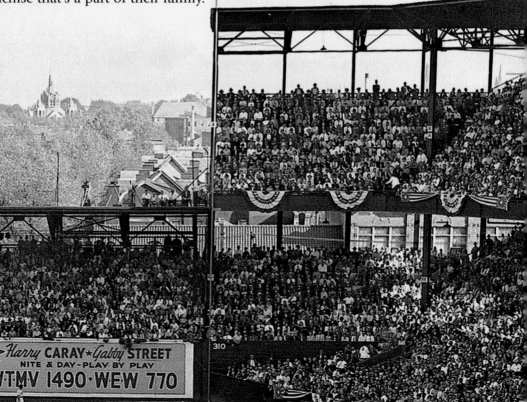

310

Griesedieck Bros. LIGHT LAGER BEER

→ Harry CARAY ★ Gabby STREET
NITE & DAY · PLAY BY PLAY
WTMV 1490 · WEW 770

1 The Birds on the Bat

The image of a franchise and a nation of fans.

2 Before They Were Cardinals

They weren't always the Cardinals. They were the Brown Stockings in 1882 in the American Association. Then they became the Browns from 1883 to 1898 in the American Association, the brief Union Association, and, finally, in 1892, the National League. After Cardinal red was added to the uniforms, they were the Perfectos for a year, in 1899, before becoming the Cardinals.

3 Chris Von der Ahe

Von der Ahe set the early standard for flamboyance as an owner. In the late 1890s, when the team was still known as the Browns, he had water slides at the ballpark, beer gardens, a horse track, and Wild West shows.

The players would ride wagons to the game, which were pulled by horses draped in blankets bearing the Browns' name. Von der Ahe, wearing a top hat and overcoat, and with a greyhound on each side of him, would lead the team in a parade around the ballpark before the game.

VON DER AHE - PRESIDENT ST. LOUIS

Albert Pujols

4 The Nickname

"Cardinals" comes from the distinctive and almost instantly recognizable color of the uniform trim. When brothers Frank de Haas Robison and Stan Robison bought the team in 1899, they added red socks to the new uniforms, which prompted *St. Louis Republic* sportswriter William McHale to call the team the Cardinals.

5 The Interlocking StL on the Cap

It's instantly recognizable: a big S, a smaller T, and a big L, laid over one another to create a symbol that identifies the city and the region where baseball is rooted in people's the souls.

Sportsman's Park

6 League Park

Von der Ahe's park, renamed when he sold the team, is where St. Louis baseball took root. From 1893 to 1920 (with the exception of 1901), the Browns, the Perfectos, and the Cardinals played there.

7 Sportsman's Park

From 1920 to 1953, the Cardinals shared Sportsman's Park with the St. Louis Browns. When brewing magnate Gussie Busch bought the ballpark from the Browns in 1953, he intended to name his acquisition "Budweiser Stadium." National League officials didn't like the idea and convinced him, instead, to name it Busch Stadium. Among its features was a large Anheuser-Busch eagle sign that flapped its wings when a Cardinal player hit a home run. The Cardinals played here until May 8, 1966, at which point they had a helicopter carry home plate to the new Busch Memorial Stadium.

3-Finger Brown, 1914, as a member of the St. Louis Federals

8 The Bet

In an unfortunate show of bravado on April 23, 1902, Cardinals owner Frank de Haas Robison bet the Pittsburgh Pirates $10,000 that they would not repeat as National League champions. The Pirates players scraped together $10,000 and took the bet. The Pirates won the pennant by 27 1/2 games.

9 Mordecai "3-Finger" Brown

The Hall of Fame pitcher, so nicknamed because he lost part of his index finger and mangled his middle finger in a farm accident in his youth, played only one season for St. Louis. Despite a 2.60 earned run average in 1903, the Cardinals traded Brown to the Cubs for pitcher Jack Taylor and catcher Larry McLean. It wasn't the greatest trade in Cardinals history, but the team made up for it 61 years later by getting Lou Brock from the Cubs for Ernie Broglio.

"To know for sure, I'd have to throw with a normal hand, and I've never tried it."

—Mordecai "3-Finger" Brown, when asked if his curve was helped by the absence of an index finger

10 Mrs. H.H. Britton

Helen Hathaway Britton became the owner of the St. Louis Cardinals in 1911 after her uncle, Stan Robison, died; she renamed the ballpark Robison Field. According to published reports, Britton became the first woman ever to sit in on a major-league baseball meeting when she attended the National League meetings at New York's Waldorf-Astoria Hotel on December 13, 1911.

11 Great Names

Ody Abbott, Skeeter Barnes, Zinn Beck, Coonie Blank, Buster Brown, Count Campau, Hick Carpenter, Cupid Childs, Creepy Crespi, Pea Ridge Day, Wheezer Dell, Pickles Dillhoefer, Klondike Douglass, Mudcat Grant, Pink Hawley, Dummy Hoy, Bubber Jonnard, Chick King, Silver King, Clyde Kluttz, Peanuts Lowrey, Rabbit Maranville, Wally Moon, Rebel Oakes, Cotton Pippen, Preacher Roe, Epp Sell, Speed Walker, Possum Whitted, Steamboat Williams, Ivey Wingo, and the Davises: Daisy, Jumbo, Kiddo, and Spud.

Schuyler and Helen Hathaway Britton

12 Miller Huggins

Huggins spent much of his playing career as a player-manager for the Cardinals, where he was a second baseman. Huggins played for the Cardinals from 1910 to 1916 and managed the team from 1913 through 1917. Known as "the Mighty Mite" because he was only 5'6", Huggins developed into a legendary manager, thanks in part to his early years in St. Louis. He ultimately led the New York Yankees to six American League pennants and three World Series titles.

"A good catcher is the quarterback, the carburetor, the lead dog, the pulse taker, the traffic cop, and sometimes a lot of unprintable things, but no team gets very far without one."

—Miller Huggins

Roger Bressnahan

13 The Train Wreck

The Cardinals were traveling to Boston on July 11, 1911, when the Federal Express train of the New York, New Haven and Hartford Railroad they were on plunged down an 18-foot embankment near Bridgeport, Connecticut. Fourteen passengers were killed. The Cardinals helped remove the bodies and aided the injured victims at the scene of the accident.

During the trip, the Cardinals had changed cars, moving from near the front of the train to get away from the noise that made it difficult to sleep. The car the Cardinals had been traveling in was crushed in the accident.

14 Roger Bresnahan

Bresnahan was a Hall of Fame catcher who managed and caught for the Cardinals from 1909 through 1912. His greatest contribution to the game lives on today: he's the guy credited with inventing shin guards for catchers.

"Roger is a fighter; he was a fighter when a pupil of [John] McGraw's and he has instilled this fighting spirit into his team."

—Fred Lieb, *Baseball Magazine*, 1911

15 Branch Rickey

One of baseball's great visionaries, Rickey played three seasons for the St. Louis Browns and later managed the Browns (1913–15) and the Cardinals (1919–25). He remained a club executive until 1942.

Rickey's greatest impact came as a baseball executive: he helped create the farm system, introduced batting helmets, made statistics a central element in the game, and, in 1945, broke baseball's color barrier by signing Jackie Robinson to play for the Brooklyn Dodgers.

"Trade a player a year too early rather than a year too late."

—Branch Rickey

Joe "Ducky" Medwick and Branch Rickey

16 The Farm System

It has been a part of baseball for nearly a century now, but it began in the Cardinals organization under Branch Rickey. In small towns throughout the heartland, the Cardinals' farm system grew into an extraordinary web of minor-league teams tied to the big club. At one point, the Cardinals had more than 25 teams in their farm system.

"He could recognize a great player from the window of a moving train."

—Jim Murray on Branch Rickey

17 Rogers Hornsby

When the subject is great right-handed hitters, Hornsby's name is near the top of the list. He played for the Cardinals from 1915 through 1926, eventually ending up at second base, and returned for a time in 1933. He also managed the Cardinals in 1925–26, leading them to their first World Series title in 1926. Hornsby was a two-time National League Most Valuable Player (1925, 1929), and his .359 career batting average is still the highest in NL history.

18 The Rajah's Run

Hornsby won seven National League batting titles, including six in a row. During his remarkable run, Hornsby—nicknamed "Rajah"—hit over .400 three times. In winning six straight batting titles, Hornsby hit:

1920: .370
1921: .397
1922: .401
1923: .384
1924: .424
1925: .403

"The home run became glorified with Babe Ruth. Starting with him, batters have been thinking in terms of how far they could hit the ball, not how often."

—Rogers Hornsby

19 Sunny Jim's Sunny Day

On September 16, 1924, Sunny Jim Bottomley went 6-for-6 with 12 runs batted in, in a win over the Brooklyn Dodgers. Bottomley was the 1928 National League MVP, when he led the league in triples, home runs (tied with Hack Wilson), and RBI.

Jim Bottomley, second row, far left, leaning forward; Rogers Hornsby, second row, fifth from right with crossed arms; Grover Cleveland Alexander, front row, far right.

20 1926: The First World Series Title

After playing its last 24 games on the road, St. Louis wound up facing the 1926 New York Yankees in the World Series. In the decisive Game 7 at Yankee Stadium, Grover Cleveland Alexander (who had started and won Games 2 and 6) pitched 21/3 shutout innings in relief to nail down the 3–2 victory. The game ended when Babe Ruth was caught trying to steal second in the bottom of the ninth with cleanup hitter Bob Meusel at the plate, ending the final Yankees threat.

"It's a beautiful day for a night game."

—Frankie Frisch

21 Frankie Frisch

Nicknamed "the Fordham Flash" in college for his speed, Frisch batted .316 in his career, with 2,880 hits and 419 stolen bases. The National League MVP in 1931, Frisch hit the first NL home run in the first All-Star Game in 1933. He also managed the famous Gas House Gang.

22 Jesse "Pop" Haines

A Hall of Famer, Haines pitched 18 seasons for the Cardinals, winning 210 times. His 554 appearances are the most ever by a St. Louis pitcher.

"When I saw how hard a nice old man like Pop could take it after losing a game I realized why he'd been a consistent winner and the Cardinals, too."

—Terry Moore

Pop Haines

23 Pepper Martin

He was called "the Wild Horse of the Osage" and was one of the characters in the Gas House Gang. Legend has it that Pepper literally didn't wear anything under his uniform when he played baseball.

Martin's performance in the 1931 World Series still ranks among the top individual accomplishments in the Fall Classic. In a Series victory over the Philadelphia Athletics, Martin batted .500, going 12 for 24, and had five RBI, scored five runs, and stole five bases.

24 The Mudcat Band

This hillbilly music group included Pepper Martin (who sometimes wore a grass skirt) on harmonica and guitar; Lon Warneke on guitar; Bob Weiland on the jug; Frenchy Bordagaray on the washboard, whistle, and car horn; and Bill McGee on the fiddle. The Mudcat Band was good enough to perform on the radio; among its more popular tunes was "Possum Up a Gum Stump."

A policeman pretends to reprimand Pepper Martin for speeding before Game 3 of the World Series, 1931

Dizzy Dean,
Daffy Dean,
Frankie Frisch,
and Bill DeLancey

25 The Gas House Gang

In the midst of the Great Depression, the 1934 Cardinals gave St. Louis—and all of baseball—one of its most colorful teams. With a circus-like collection of characters that included Dizzy Dean, Pepper Martin, Leo Durocher, Frankie Frisch, Paul "Daffy" Dean, and Joe "Ducky" Medwick, the Gas House Gang played its way into history.

Trailing the New York Giants by 5 1/2 games in mid-September, the Gas House Gang rallied to win the National League pennant, then beat the Detroit Tigers to win the World Series.

"A chunky, unshaven hobo who ran the bases like a berserk locomotive, slept in the raw, and swore at pitchers in his sleep."

—Lee Allen on Pepper Martin

26 Leo Durocher

Leo the Lip was one of the loud, flamboyant members of the Gas House Gang. Because of the way he used to run his mouth, inciting and antagonizing umpires and opposing players, he was never the most popular guy in the game. A pool shark, Durocher gave the game one of its enduring adages when he said nice guys finish last.

27 The Other Babe

The great Babe Didrikson was a Cardinal for a day. On March 22, 1934, she pitched one inning for the Cardinals in a spring-training game against the Boston Red Sox. Didrikson surrendered four hits and three runs in her only inning on the mound. She was not, however, the first female to play for a major-league team. That honor belonged to first baseman Lizzie Murphy, who played for an American League all-star team in an exhibition game in 1922.

Babe Didrikson

28 Dizzy Dean

There was no one quite like Ol' Diz. He could fire bullets past batters and averaged 24 wins a season over his first five full seasons in the big leagues. He was a strikeout king, too, leading the National League in Ks four straight years. But he was more than just a pitcher. Dizzy Dean was a cultural classic, blending down-home humor with beaming personality to become a huge star.

29 According to Dizzy

Among the gems that came from Dizzy Dean:

"Anybody who's ever had the privilege of seeing me play knows that I am the greatest pitcher in the world."

"I ain't what I used to be, but who the hell is?"

"It ain't braggin' if you can back it up."

"It puzzles me how they know what corners are good for filling stations. Just how did they know gas and oil was under there?"

"The Good Lord was good to me. He gave me a strong body, a good right arm, and a weak mind."

30 Paul "Daffy" Dean

Dizzy's brother was also a Cardinals pitcher, though he lacked his brother's crackling personality. When Paul joined the Cardinals in 1934, Dizzy predicted they would win 45 games between them. He was wrong. They won 49 — 30 of them by Dizzy.

31 Brothers in Arms

On September 21, 1934, with the Cardinals in a pennant race, the Dean brothers pitched both ends of a doubleheader against the Dodgers. In the opener, Dizzy shut out the Dodgers on three hits. In the nightcap, brother Paul threw a no-hitter. Afterward, Dizzy remarked, "I wish I'da known Paul was goin' to pitch a no-hitter. I'da pitched one, too."

"They X-rayed my head and didn't find anything."

—Dizzy Dean after being hit in the head by a baseball

Dizzy Dean, Grover Cleveland Alexander, Daffy Dean

32 Walter Alston

Although the great manager earned his spot in the Hall of Fame because of his success on the bench with the Los Angeles Dodgers, Alston had one memorable moment as a member of the Cardinals: he got his only major-league at bat in 1936. Alston struck out.

33 The Big Cat

Johnny "Big Cat" Mize played first base for the Cardinals from 1936 through 1941 and was a 10-time All-Star in his career (four times as a Cardinal). A great power hitter, with 359 career home runs, Mize hit three home runs in a game six times.

Don Padgett, Johnny Mize, Enos Slaughter, and Terry Moore

> "I'd rather pitch to any other hitter in the league. He's bad news all the time. No game is ever won against the Cardinals until [Joe] Medwick is out in the ninth."
>
> —Van Mungo

Joe "Ducky" Medwick

34 Joe "Ducky" Medwick

Another Cardinals Hall of Famer, Ducky won the National League MVP award and the Triple Crown in 1937—the last time an NL player won the Triple Crown. A lifetime .324 hitter, Medwick earned his nickname for his waddling walk. A tough, gruff left fielder, Medwick was part of the famous Gas House Gang.

Charlie Gehringer and
Joe Medwick

35 39 Plaques

That's how many former Cardinals are in the Baseball Hall of Fame. For the record, they're Grover Cleveland Alexander, Walter Alston, Jake Beckley, Sunny Jim Bottomley, Roger Bresnahan, Lou Brock, Mordecai Brown, Jesse Burkett, Steve Carlton, Orlando Cepeda, Roger Connor, Dizzy Dean, Leo Durocher, Dennis Eckersley, Frankie Frisch, Pud Galvin, Bob Gibson, and Burleigh Grimes.

And Chick Hafey, Jesse Haines, Rogers Hornsby, Miller Huggins, Rabbit Maranville, John McGraw, Bill McKechnie, Joe Medwick, Johnny Mize, Stan Musial, Kid Nichols, Branch Rickey, Wilbert Robinson, Red Schoendienst, Enos Slaughter, Ozzie Smith, Dazzy Vance, Bobby Wallace, Hoyt Wilhelm, Vic Willis, and Cy Young.

36 15 Consecutive Winning Seasons

From 1939 through 1953, the Cardinals finished over .500 every year. In eight of those seasons, they won more than 90 games.

"How does one express the indescribable feeling of finally reaching this summit that so many others have struggled to obtain, but fell short of achieving?"

—from Ozzie Smith's Hall of Fame induction speech

OSBORNE EARL SMITH
"Ozzie" "The Wizard"

Terry Moore bats in
the 1942 World Series

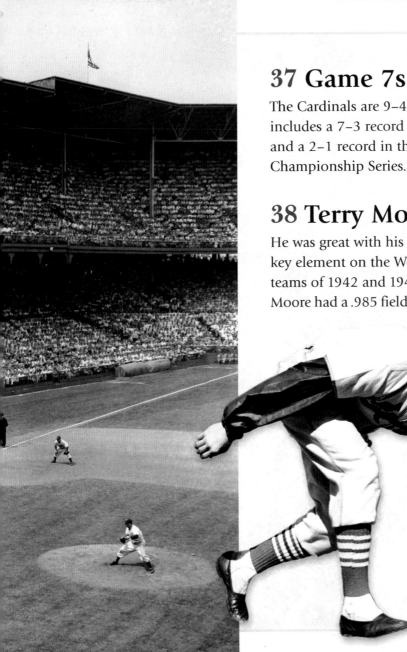

37 Game 7s

The Cardinals are 9–4 in ultimate games. That includes a 7–3 record in World Series Game 7s and a 2–1 record in the National League Championship Series.

38 Terry Moore

He was great with his glove in center field and a key element on the World Series championship teams of 1942 and 1946. A career .280 hitter, Moore had a .985 fielding percentage.

39 Stan "the Man" Musial

He is the face of Cardinals baseball. Musial earned
his nickname in Brooklyn when Dodgers fans
were overheard saying, "Oh no, here comes the
Man again," as Musial stepped to the plate. With
Musial in the lineup, the Cardinals won three
World Series and four pennants in the 1940s.

Musial began his career as a pitcher and went 18–5
at Daytona Beach, but he hurt his shoulder in a
fall during spring training. The Cardinals decided
to try him in the outfield, and, after that, nothing
was ever the same.

*"I don't think there is anyone in any sport
who combined the supreme talent with
a great personality. He is also one of the
most beautiful people who ever walked
the face of the earth. I don't think there's
anybody who compares to Stan Musial
on both fronts."*

—Jack Buck

40 The Man's Doubleheader

On August 11, 1946, Musial went 8-for-9 in a doubleheader sweep of the Cincinnati Reds. The next day, Musial went 4-for-4, making him 12-for-13 in two days.

41 The Man's Other Doubleheader

On May 2, 1954, Musial clobbered five home runs in a doubleheader against the New York Giants.

42 The Man's Numbers

Musial's Hall of Fame numbers are only part of his story. He was hugely popular and played the game with the uncommon grace that the great ones have. The numbers, though, are remarkable:
- 3,630 career base hits
- 1,815 hits on the road, 1,815 hits at home
- 24 All-Star Game appearances
- 6 All-Star Game home runs
- 475 career home runs
- 7 National League batting titles
- 17 straight seasons with an average of .300 or better

43 Youth Day

On June 10, 1944, the Cardinals gave young Joe Nuxhall of the Cincinnati Reds a lesson in experience. Nuxhall was only 15 years and 10 months old when he pitched in the last inning against the Cardinals, surrendering five runs on five walks and two hits, while recording only two outs, in what would end up an 18–0 St. Louis victory.

44 Spring Training

For nearly 60 years, the Cardinals spent their springs in St. Petersburg, Florida, where everything seemed possible. Before the pressure of the regular season arrived, the Cardinals trained in the relaxed sunshine at a ballpark surrounded by palm trees and saltwater. The Cardinals have held spring training in Jupiter, Florida, at Roger Dean Stadium, since 1998, maintaining the special feeling of springtime and the hope it brings to each baseball team.

45 A Great Finishing Kick

While the world was at war, the 1942 Cardinals produced one of the great runs in baseball history. They won 41 of their last 48 games, going 21–4 in September, to win the National League title with a franchise-record 106 victories. When Whitey Kurowski hammered a two-run homer in the top of the ninth of Game 5 against the Yankees, another world championship arrived in St. Louis.

46 316

For three years, the Cardinals won baseball games as if they owned them. In 1942, the Cardinals won 106 games; then they won 105 in each of the next two seasons. Put it together and they went 316–146, a winning percentage of .684 over three years, while taking two World Series (1942, 1944) in the process.

"In '42 we played together and fought together.... We had that Cardinal spirit; we thought we could beat anybody and we did."

—Stan Musial

47 Mort Cooper

He was the 1942 National League MVP after posting a 22–7 record with a 1.78 ERA. In a three-year stretch starting in 1942, Cooper had a 65–22 record. Despite the death of their father, Mort and his brother, Walker, were the winning battery in Game 2 of the 1943 World Series.

Cooper wore number 13, but with each start he made in 1942, he exchanged his jersey with the teammate who wore the number that corresponded to the victory he was going for, working his way up from 1 all the way to 22.

48 The One-Hit Wonder

Mort Cooper pitched back-to-back one-hitters in 1943. The first came in a victory over the Brooklyn Dodgers on May 31. It was followed by another one-hit victory, over the Philadelphia Phillies, on June 4.

Marty Marion

49 The Trolley Car Series

In 1944, the Cardinals met their rivals and American League parkmates, the St. Louis Browns, in the World Series. Every game was played in Sportsman's Park, and the Cardinals won the Series in six games. It was the Cardinals' eighth Series appearance in 19 years, but the only time in the 52-year history of the Browns that they made it that far.

50 Marty Marion

Before there was Ozzie Smith at shortstop, there was Marty Marion. "The Octopus" was amazing defensively, posting a .969 career fielding percentage. Marion was so good that he won the National League MVP in 1944, by one vote over the Cubs' Bill Nicholson, despite batting eighth and hitting just .267 with only 63 RBI.

Marion played the 1944 World Series with a fever of 104 while suffering from the flu. His wife wasn't there to care for him. She had gone home to give birth to their second child. Marion later said, "I played every game, but as soon as the game was over, I'd go back and get in bed, and for three days all I had was orange juice. I didn't tell nobody. Nobody knew I was sick."

51 Enos "Country" Slaughter

A great player for many years, Slaughter cemented his place in history with one play, in Game 7 of the 1946 World Series. With the Cardinals locked in a tie game with Boston, Slaughter scored the Series-winning run from first base on a double by Harry Walker — a play that became known as "Slaughter's Mad Dash." Slaughter hit .300 or better 10 times in his career. At his funeral, his daughters sang "Take Me Out to the Ball Game."

Enos Slaughter scoring in a game versus Brooklyn

52 The Retired Numbers

 1 Ozzie Smith
 2 Red Schoendienst
 6 Stan Musial
 9 Enos Slaughter
14 Ken Boyer
17 Dizzy Dean
20 Lou Brock
45 Bob Gibson
85 August Busch

Plus flags for announcer Jack Buck and Jackie Robinson.

53 Butch Yatkeman

For more than five decades (1924–82), Yatkeman was the Cardinals' clubhouse attendant. He was also the only man who was part of all nine Cardinals world championships.

54 Under the Lights

On April 18, 1950, what has traditionally been called Opening Day was, for the first time, Opening Night. The Cardinals hosted the Pittsburgh Pirates in the first season-opener played under the lights. The Cardinals won, 4–2.

55 KMOX

For over five decades, it has been the radio lifeline of the Cardinals. With its signal reaching throughout the heartland and into the South, the Cardinals became a daily part of life for thousands who were nowhere near the ballpark. However, word came in August 2005 that the 52-year run would end after the season, with broadcasts shifting to KTRS.

"I listened to him and Harry Caray when I was growing up. Most people were Harry Caray fans, but I was more of a Jack Buck fan.... He was the fan's eyes to the game and described what they wanted to hear."

—Bill Brown

Jack Buck and Albert Pujols

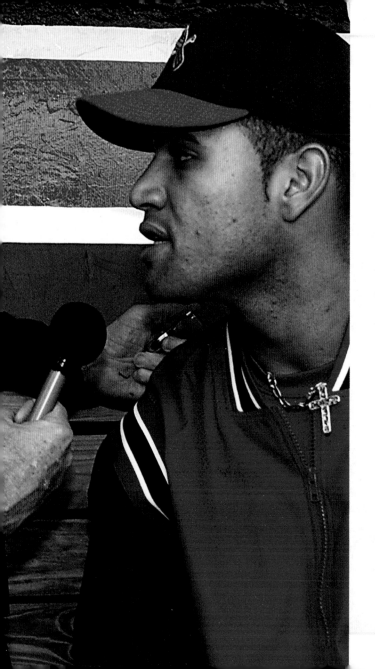

56 Jack Buck

For nearly 50 years, Jack Buck's voice was as much a part of the franchise as the team colors. From 1954 through 2001, Buck worked first as a color man on radio broadcasts with Harry Caray and then, starting in 1970, as the play-by-play man. A great citizen of St. Louis, Buck became the 11th broadcaster honored by the Hall of Fame with its Ford C. Frick Award.

"That's a winner."

—Jack Buck

"If a guy hits .300 every year, what does he have to look forward to? I always tried to stay around .190, with three or four RBI. And I tried to get them all in September. That way I always had something to talk about during the winter."

—Bob Uecker

57 Red Schoendienst

He so wanted to be a St. Louis Cardinal that, the story goes, he slept on a park bench outside the St. Louis train station the night before his tryout. Schoendienst earned his Hall of Fame spot as a player and manager. A second baseman, Schoendienst led the league in fielding percentage seven times and had a remarkable .982 fielding percentage in his career. As a manager, he led the Cardinals to the 1967 world championship.

58 Bob Uecker

He was with the Cardinals for only a short time (1964–65), but Uecker kept his teammates laughing while he was there. While posing for the 1964 team photo, Uecker convinced tough guy Bob Gibson to hold his hand. When team officials later discovered the prank, the photo was reshot.

Red Schoendienst

59 1964

Eleven games behind Philadelphia in the National League on August 24, the Cardinals took advantage of the Phillies' collapse and wound up winning the World Series over the Yankees.

60 September 13, 1964

The Cardinals achieved a baseball rarity by scoring in all nine innings against the Cubs.

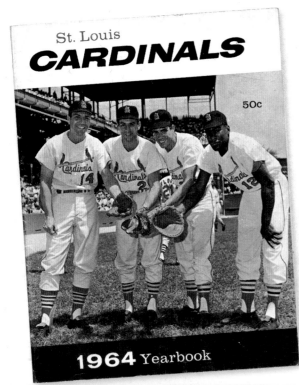

Tim McCarver, Ken Boyer, and Bob Gibson celebrate winning the 1964 World Series

61 Curt Flood

In his own way, Flood changed baseball. He was an excellent outfielder, once playing 226 consecutive games without making an error. In six different seasons, Flood batted .300 or better. His lasting impact, however, came off the field, when he challenged baseball's reserve clause in 1970 after he was traded to Philadelphia. Flood refused to play for the Phillies and ultimately sat out the season. He lost his court case seeking to overturn baseball's antitrust exemption but, down the road, his efforts led to the arrival of free agency.

"Dear Mr. Kuhn,
After twelve years in the major leagues, I do not feel I am a piece of property to be bought and sold irrespective of my wishes."

—Curt Flood

62 Ken Boyer

He was an anchor at third base, where he won five Gold Gloves and picked up the 1964 MVP award. Originally drafted as a pitcher, Boyer was a 10-time All-Star who had a knack for the big moment. In the 1964 World Series, he smashed a grand slam in the sixth inning of Game 4 at Yankee Stadium and hit another home run in Game 7.

Boyer's brother Clete, who played third base for the Yankees, also hit a home run in Game 7, the only time brothers have hit home runs in the same World Series game.

63 Larry Jaster

In 1966, Jaster made five starts against the eventual National League champion Los Angeles Dodgers. Jaster pitched five shutouts, allowing just 24 singles in 45 innings pitched.

Larry Jaster

"The ballplayers know he's a good one, but nobody else does."

—Stan Musial on Ken Boyer

Tim McCarver

64 Mike "Moon Man" Shannon

Beloved as the Cardinals third baseman in the 1960s, Shannon is equally beloved as a color commentator on the KMOX broadcasts.

65 Harry Caray

Holy cow! Did you know that before the Cubs, Caray called games for the Cardinals?

66 The Voices

Among the Cardinals who went on to be successful announcers: Dizzy Dean, Joe Garagiola, Bob Uecker, Tim McCarver, Bill White, Bob Tewksbury, Joe Torre, Joe Magrane, Al Hrabosky, and Jim Kaat.

Mike Shannon

"The wind has shifted 360 degrees."

—Mike Shannon

67 Busch Stadium

In its five decades of existence, Busch Stadium has been at the heart of the Cardinals' story. Not only did it help revitalize downtown St. Louis, but it became one of the most recognizable stadiums in the world. With its 96 distinctive arches around the top rim of the stadium — built to resemble the nearby Gateway Arch — Busch Stadium opened in 1966 and closed at the end of the 2005 season, having earned a place among the most famous ballparks in history.

"There's a full moon over Busch Stadium tonight. We hope there's a full moon where you are, too."

—Mike Shannon

68 The New Ballpark

The Cardinals took ownership of their new home, adjacent to Busch Stadium, as the 2006 season began. With a classic design that brings together the old and the new, the park keeps alive the history of the Cardinals while offering dramatic views of the Gateway Arch and the St. Louis skyline. It is also called Busch Stadium.

69 The Clydesdales

The famous Budweiser horses were regulars at Cardinals games when the Busch family owned the team.

An architectural rendering of the new Busch Stadium

70 Bob Gibson

He was the personification of toughness on the mound. Gibson's glaring demeanor on the hill, coupled with his power, made him one of the most intimidating pitchers of his time or any other.

How tough was Gibson? During a 1967 game against the Pirates, Roberto Clemente hit a line drive that broke Gibson's leg. Gibson pitched to three more batters before leaving the game. Gibson was a such a gifted athlete that he played for a time for basketball's Harlem Globetrotters.

71 Gibson by the Numbers

Among the highlights of Gibson's career:
- His 1.12 ERA in 1968 is the lowest since 1914.
- Gibson won the National League Cy Young and MVP awards in 1968, when he went 22–9 with 13 shutouts and 28 complete games.
- He also won the 1970 Cy Young award.
- He finished with 251 wins, 3,117 strikeouts, and a lifetime ERA of 2.91.

"He could throw a baseball through a brick wall."

—Curt Flood

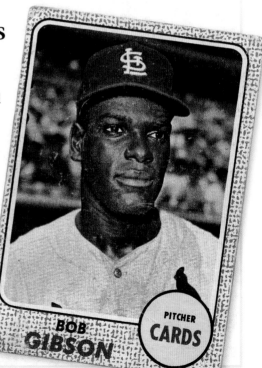

BOB GIBSON

PITCHER CARDS

72 Gibson's 1967 World Series

Upon returning from a broken leg suffered earlier in the season, Gibson dominated the 1967 World Series. In Game 1 against the Red Sox, Gibson had 10 strikeouts in a 2–1 victory. In Game 4, Gibson pitched a five-hit shutout. In Game 7, Gibson once again struck out 10, and hit a home run, in a 7–2 St. Louis victory.

73 Lonborg and Champagne

On the morning of Game 7 in the 1967 World Series, the *Boston Record American* newspaper ran a headline that read, "Lonborg and Champagne," a reference to Bosox starter Jim Lonborg, who was pitching the finale, in anticipation of the Red Sox ending their long history of World Series frustration. The Cardinals took notice, and during their championship celebration after a 7–2 victory, they chanted, "Lonborg and champagne, hey!"

"I remember one time going out to the mound to talk with Bob Gibson. He told me to get back behind the batter, that the only thing I knew about pitching was that it was hard to hit."

—Tim McCarver

Orlando Cepeda and
Carl Yastrzemski

74 Cha Cha

Orlando Cepeda's short stint with the Cardinals was highlighted by his MVP season in 1967 when he provided the muscle in a world championship season. Cepeda batted .325, hit 25 home runs, and drove in 111 runs in the best season of a Hall of Fame career.

Joe Torre

75 Bob Forsch

It might be enough to say Forsch pitched two no-hitters for the Cardinals, but that wouldn't really say it all about him. Look down the list of Cardinals pitching records; Forsch's name is sprinkled throughout. Games pitched, wins, strikeouts—all the things that matter most have Forsch's name included high on the list.

76 Joe Torre

By hitting .363 and driving in 137 runs, Torre was the National League MVP in 1971. Never blessed with speed but instead with an instinctive understanding of how the game should be played, Torre was a terrific team player. Pirates shortstop Gene Alley once joked that Torre hit the ball so hard that had he been faster he could have batted .400. Torre managed the Cardinals from 1990–95 and went on from there to guide the New York Yankees to four World Series titles between 1996 and 2000.

"Winning is more likely to create team unity than vice versa."

—Joe Torre

77 Lou Brock

He was the essence of speed and team play in his Cardinals career. Brock is best known for his base-stealing talents. He stole a major-league-record 118 bases in 1974, breaking Maury Wills' single-season record, and Brock finished his career with 938 stolen bases. Brock was seemingly always on base, compiling 3,023 career hits. He excelled in the postseason, too, with a .391 career batting average in three World Series.

"*Show me a guy who's afraid to look bad, and I'll show you a guy you can beat every time.*"

—Lou Brock

78 Keith Hernandez

Hernandez shared the 1979 National League MVP award with Pittsburgh's Willie Stargell. A first baseman who won five straight Gold Glove awards with the Cardinals (and 11 straight overall), Hernandez also carved out a piece of pop-culture history when he played himself in an episode of *Seinfeld* in which he befriended Jerry, dated Elaine, and was the subject of a conspiracy theory involving Kramer.

"Acting is really not what I'm interested in. I'm not an aspiring actor and you should be able to tell."

—Keith Hernandez

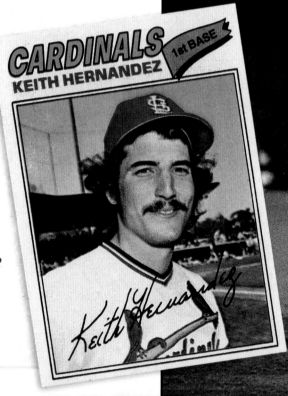

79 Willie McGee

The Cardinals sent Bob Sykes into oblivion with the New York Yankees and wound up with Willie McGee, in one of the best trades in team history. He set the Cardinals in motion with his speed, which helped characterize the club. In the 1982 World Series, McGee hit two home runs and robbed Milwaukee's Gorman Thomas of a dinger in Game 3.

80 Stealing Home

Glenn Brummer was a slow backup catcher who would never be a threat to steal a base, particularly home with the bases loaded and two outs in the bottom of the twelfth inning. But that's what Brummer did against the San Francisco Giants on August 22, 1982, giving the Cardinals a 5–4 victory and earning a place in Cardinals fans' hearts forever. One of only four stolen bases in Brummer's 178-game major-league career, it was a daring move that surprised everyone, including his teammates and coaches.

"A guy told me he was listening to the radio and drove off the road. Another guy told me he was barbecuing and knocked his grill over. I guess they haven't forgotten."

—Glenn Brummer

81 Whiteyball

Manager Whitey Herzog reshaped the
Cardinals in the 1980s, bringing in Ozzie
Smith, Bruce Sutter, and Darrell Porter,
among others. Herzog, who directed the
Cardinals to three NL pennants and
one world championship in 11 years,
emphasized speed on the bases, great
defense, and an unorthodox approach to
the game that kept opponents off balance.

82 Ted Simmons

When the subject turns to great catchers,
Simmons belongs in the conversation. His
career batting average of .285 was higher
than those of greats Johnny Bench, Carlton
Fisk, Gary Carter, and Roy Campanella
(and tied with Yogi Berra's). He also had
more hits and doubles than any of those
catchers and more RBI than all but Berra.
Cardinals fans will also tell you he belongs
in the Hall of Fame.

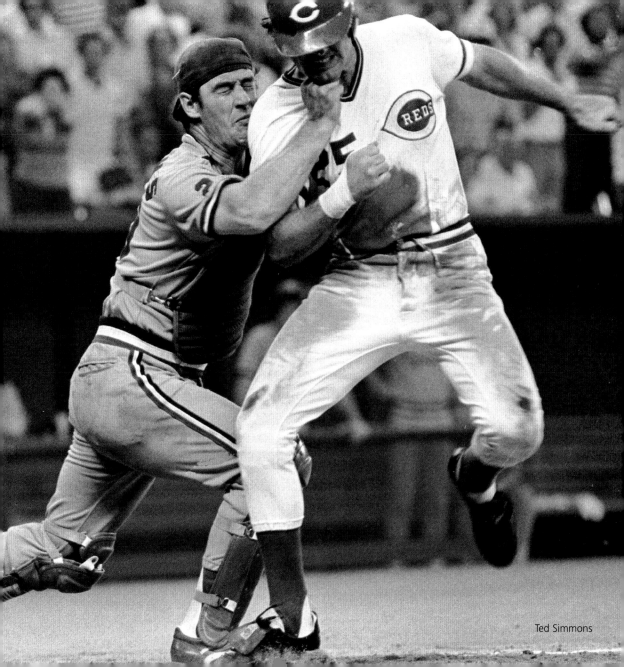

Ted Simmons

83 The Wizard of Oz

Ozzie Smith redefined how to play shortstop. Blessed with remarkable quickness, agility, and instincts, Smith owned the position. He won 13 consecutive Gold Glove awards and captured the imagination of fans everywhere in the same way great power hitters do. Before postseason games, Smith would do a backflip while taking the field; then he would do magic with his glove. A Hall of Famer, Smith had 2,460 hits and 580 stolen bases while setting a variety of records for fielding by a shortstop.

"Giving back is the ultimate talent in life. That is the greatest trophy on my mantel."

—Ozzie Smith

84 One Swing

Switch-hitting Ozzie Smith had batted left-handed 3,008 times in the major leagues without hitting a home run when he stepped into the batter's box against Tom Niedenfuer of the Los Angeles Dodgers in the bottom of the ninth in Game 5 of the 1985 National League Championship Series. Smith homered off Niedenfuer to win the game and put the Cardinals up in the series 3 games to 2.

85 Jack Clark's Home Run

Two days after teammate Ozzie Smith hit a home run off Los Angeles Dodgers reliever Tom Niedenfuer, Jack Clark stepped into the batter's box at Dodger Stadium with two outs in the ninth inning of Game 6 in the 1985 NLCS. With the Cardinals trailing and a base open, Dodgers manager Tommy Lasorda decided to pitch to Clark rather than intentionally walk him. Facing Niedenfuer, Clark ripped a three-run homer over the left-field wall to win the game. Left fielder Pedro Guerrero immediately knew it was gone, just turning to watch it, then throwing his glove down in disgust. The Cardinals won 7–5 and took the series 4–2.

"Smith corks one into right down the line. It may go! Go crazy, folks, go crazy! It's a home run and the Cardinals have won the game by the score of 3–2 on a home run by the Wizard!"

—Jack Buck calling Ozzie Smith's home run

Ozzie Smith

Jack Clark

Al Hrabosky

86 The I-70 Series

The 1985 World Series split the state of Missouri, with the Cardinals battling their cross-state rivals, the Kansas City Royals. The Series is remembered by Cardinals fans for "the Call." The Cardinals were leading 1–0 in the ninth inning of Game 6, needing only to close out the Royals in the inning to win the World Series, when first-base umpire Don Denkinger called Royals batter Jorge Orta safe at first. Replays subsequently showed that Orta was out. But the Royals rallied to win Game 6 and followed that by winning Game 7.

87 The Mad Hungarian

Al Hrabosky, also known as "the Mad Hungarian," had a wicked fastball, and the ability to intimidate grown men standing in the batter's box. When Hrabosky would get the call to enter a game, the Cardinals closer was serenaded by Liszt's Hungarian Rhapsody no. 2, and he worked his time on the mound like a Broadway performer, taking everyone in the park along for an unpredictable but impossible-to-ignore performance.

88 John Tudor's 1985 Season

All Tudor did was win 21 games, throw 14 complete games, lead the majors with 10 shutouts, pitch 275 innings, and post a 1.93 ERA. He also beat the Mets' Dwight Gooden in a 1–0, 10-inning September classic, but Gooden still won the Cy Young award.

89 Vince Coleman

Pure, blazing speed—that's what Coleman gave the Cardinals. In 1985, he set a rookie record with 110 stolen bases and helped run the Cardinals to the National League pennant. Coleman led the league in stolen bases six straight seasons.

90 Joaquin Andujar

No one ever knew quite what to expect from Andujar, though he won 20 games twice for the Cardinals. He showered in his clothes once after a loss and poured milk on himself another time he was beaten.

"I know he's crazy, but he really does have a heart of gold."

—Whitey Herzog on Joaquin Andujar

John Tudor

Vince Coleman

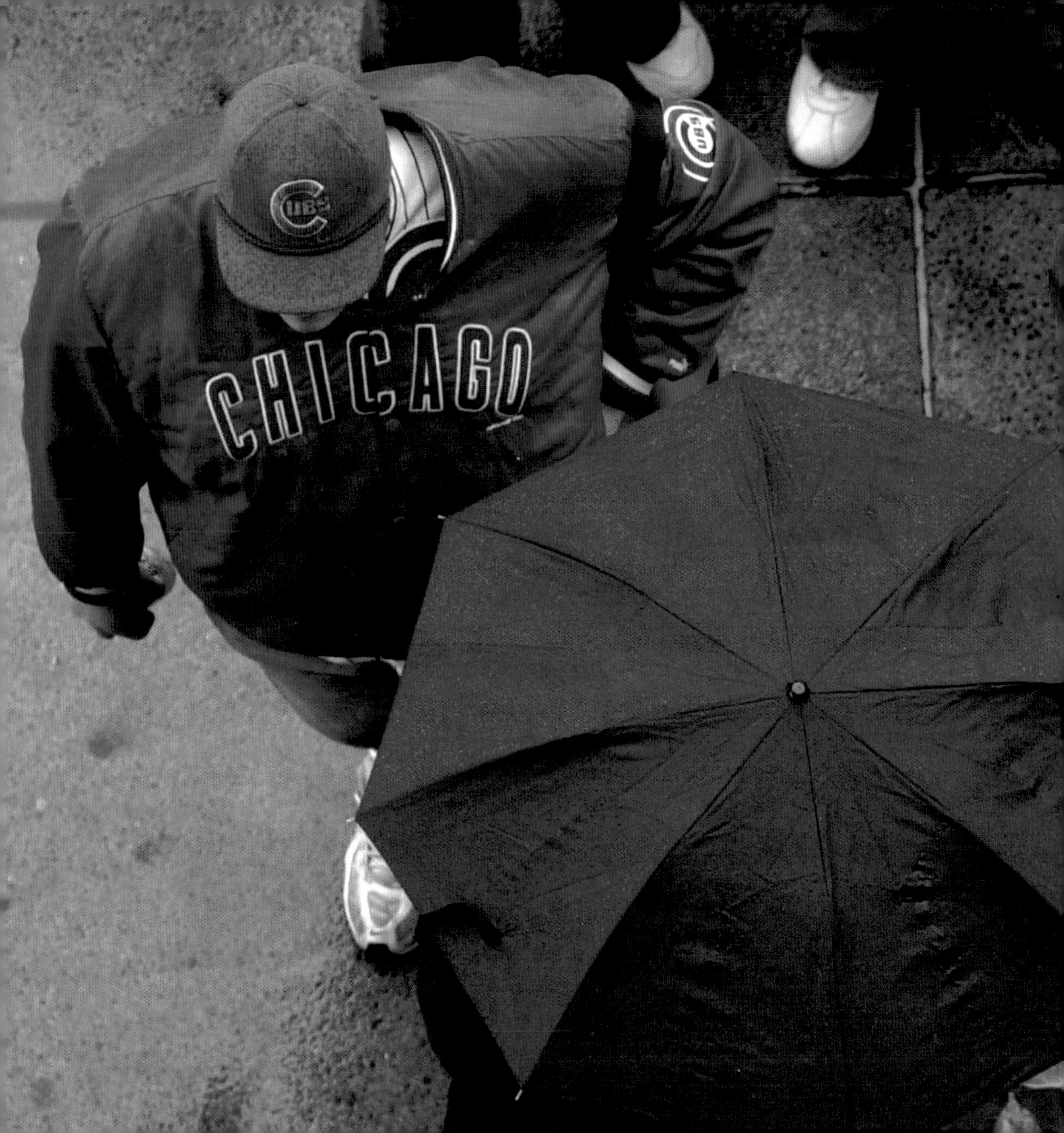
CHICAGO

91 September 7, 1993

After going hitless in the opener, Mark Whiten hit four home runs and collected 12 RBI in the second game of a doubleheader at Cincinnati.

92 The Cubs Rivalry

This is the National League version of the Yankees and the Red Sox. They're as different as the colors they wear and the cities they represent. Ultimately, it is a rivalry dominated by the Cardinals, who have been blessed with success while the Cubs have been haunted by failure.

It was somehow fitting that Stan Musial got his 3,000th career hit at Wrigley Field, and that in the midst of the great home-run chase in 1998, Mark McGwire broke Roger Maris' single-season record by clubbing his 62nd homer off Cubs pitcher Steve Trachsel. Cardinals fans know what 1908 means: the last time the Cubs won the World Series.

93 70 Home Runs

On July 31, 1997, the Cardinals sent pitchers Eric Ludwick, T.J. Mathews, and Blake Stein to Oakland for slugger Mark McGwire. In 1998, Mark McGwire shattered one of baseball's most hallowed records when he hit 70 home runs, breaking Roger Maris' long-standing record of 61. McGwire's pursuit of history coincided with a mesmerizing long-ball duel with the Chicago Cubs' Sammy Sosa, riveting the nation's attention on their achievement.

On September 8, Big Mac lasered his 62nd home run over the left-field fence to break Maris' record while Sosa watched from right field. After McGwire crossed the plate with the new record, Sosa came to greet him. McGwire hit four home runs in the last two games of the season to finish with 70.

94 Home-Run Derby

In his first three seasons with the Cardinals (including the one he started in Oakland), McGwire hit 193 home runs. That's 58, 70, 65.

95 April 23, 1999

Third baseman Fernando Tatis hit two grand slams in the same inning against the Dodgers, making him the first player ever to accomplish the feat. Tatis also set a record with eight RBI in the inning. The Cardinals defeated the Dodgers, 12–5.

96 Tony LaRussa

He's the model of modern baseball managers. They don't just tell stories about LaRussa; they write books about how he does his job. He's smart, studious, and amazingly successful. LaRussa won a division title with the Chicago White Sox in 1983, captured three American League pennants and a World Series in Oakland in 1988–90, and kept the Cardinals in the postseason with six division titles and one National League pennant between 1996 and 2004.

"Play the game right. If you play the game intelligently and execute the fundamentals, you can win."

—Tony LaRussa

97 Fans

They're the best. Unlike some other places where the fans seem to believe they're the story more than the team (the Chicago Cubs' fans come to mind), Cardinals fans are part of the franchise without turning the spotlight on themselves. They wear red, they come from all across the baseball-watching world, and they keep the Cardinals faith. That's why more than three million fans show up annually to see the Cardinals play at home.

98 John Grisham

The best-selling author is a longtime Cardinals fan. In his novel *A Painted House*, the central character is a young boy who dreams of playing for the Cardinals when he grows up. Not unlike Grisham himself.

"The first six years of my life I picked cotton, chopped cotton and worked in the fields and dreamed of playing for the Cardinals because I wasn't going to be a farmer."

—John Grisham

99 Albert Pujols

He's the new-age Musial. Few players in history have had the immediate impact that Pujols is having. Five years into his career, he has been compared to Ted Williams, Joe DiMaggio, and, of course, Stan the Man. He hit 160 home runs in his first four seasons in the big leagues, second only to Ralph Kiner's 168.

He's already done what no else ever has: Pujols is the first player to ever hit at least 30 home runs in each of his first five seasons. And it's only the start.

"He has a passion for the game, a love for the game. You can see it. You can sense it."

—Mike Easler on Albert Pujols

100 20 Pennants

Count 'em: 1885–88 (in the American Association), 1926, 1928, 1930–31, 1934, 1942–44, 1946, 1964, 1967–68, 1982, 1985, 1987, 2004.

Nine World Championships
1926, 1931, 1934, 1942, 1944, 1946, 1964, 1967, 1982. And counting.

Darrell Porter, 1982

Acknowledgments

This begins with words of thanks to Leslie Stoker and Jennifer Levesque and the other good people at Stewart, Tabori & Chang, where they understand how books enhance our lives.

Also, a special thanks to Mary Tiegreen, whose vision has led to the creation of this book and others like it. She understands the attachment that games and players have to people and places.

Thanks to Paul Gardner, a true Southern gentleman and scholar whose passion for the Cardinals runs as deep as family blood and just as red.

Again, thanks to my brother, Dave, who brought this all together and excels in the magic of creating art.

To Kevin O'Sullivan at AP/Wide World Photos, Bill Burdick and the staff at the National Baseball Hall of Fame Library, and Mellaine Burris with HOK Sport, your time and efforts are greatly appreciated.

To my wife, Tamera, and my daughter, Molly; my parents, Ron and Beth Green; my sister, Edie, and the McGlone family, as well as the Macchias and Brad Caplanides, whose allegiances range from the Phillies to the Mets, there aren't enough thanks.

And, finally, to the Cardinals and their fans who long ago figured out they were on to something special and have allowed us to enjoy it with them year after year.

A Tiegreen Book

Published in 2006 by
Stewart, Tabori & Chang
115 West 18th Street
New York, NY 10011
www.abramsbooks.com

Editor: Jennifer Levesque
Designer: David Green, Brightgreen Design
Production Manager: Kim Tyner

Library of Congress
Cataloging-in-Publication Data

Green, Ron, Jr.
  101 reasons to love the Cardinals /
Ron Green, Jr.
    p. cm.
ISBN 1-58479-498-4
1. St. Louis Cardinals (Baseball team)—
  Miscellanea.
    I. Title: One hundred one reasons
  to love the Cardinals. II. Title: One
  hundred and one reasons to love
  the Cardinals. III. Title.

GV875.S74G74 2006
796.357'64'0977866--dc22
2005024637

101 Reasons to Love the Cardinals is a book in the 101 REASONS TO LOVE™ series.

101 REASONS TO LOVE™ is a trademark of Mary Tiegreen and Hubert Pedroli.

Printed in China

10 9 8 7 6 5 4 3 2 1

First Printing

Stewart, Tabori & Chang is a subsidiary of

Photo Credits
Pages 1, 2-3, 4-5, 6-7, 10, 13, 22-23, 24, 26-27, 28, 29 (inset), 31, 32, 35, 36, 39, 40-41, 42, 45, 46, 48, 51, 52-53, 54, 56 (inset), 57, 58, 60-61, 62 (Gibson, Schoendienst, Dean, Musial, Smith, Brock, Boyer, and Busch, Jr.), 64-65, 66, 67 (inset), 69, 70, 72 (inset), 73, 74, 75 (inset), 76, 79, 80, 82, 84-85, 86, 87, 89, 91, 92, 95, 96, 98 (inset), 99, 100, 102 (inset), 103, 104, 106, 109, 110-111, 112-113, 114-115, 116-117, and 118 courtesy of AP/Wide World Photos.

Pages 50 (card), 62 (Enos Slaughter card), 71 (card), 81 (card), 90 (card), and 120 (Brock card) courtesy of David Green, Brightgreen Design.

Pages 8-9 (background/cards), 14, 16 (card), 17, 19, 20, 21(card), and 120 (Bresnahan card) courtesy of the Library of Congress Prints and Photographs Division.

Page 78 courtesy of the St. Louis Cardinals and HOK Sport + Venue + Event.

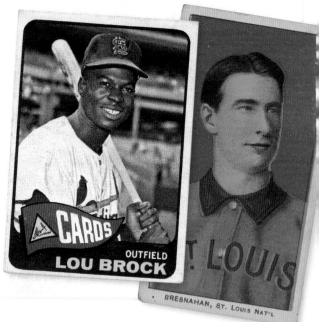